IN THE

BLEAK MIDWINTER

IN THE
BLEAK MIDWINTER

40
MEDITATIONS
AND PRAYERS

for

ADVENT AND CHRISTMAS

Herbert Brokering

Augsburg Books
Minneapolis

IN THE BLEAK MIDWINTER
Forty Meditations and Prayers for Advent and Christmas

Library of Congress Cataloging-in-Publication Data

Brokering, Herbert, 1926-
 In the bleak midwinter : forty meditations and prayers for Advent and Christmas / Herbert Brokering.
     p. cm.
 ISBN 978-0-8066-8053-8 (alk. paper)
 1. Advent—Prayers and devotions. 2. Christmas—Prayers and devotions.
 I. Title.

 BV40.B744 2008
 242'.33—dc22

                                          2008023659

Cover design by Laurie Ingram
Cover image and image on page 8: © DeA Picture Library / Art Resource, NY. Used by permission.
Book design by Christa Rubsam

Introduction

This small book of Advent devotions (with slight modification made to some of the phrasing) takes its inspiration from Christina Georgina Rossetti's poem "In the Bleak Midwinter," a well-known and well-loved Advent hymn. Rossetti wrote the poem—initially titled "A Christmas Carol"—around 1872, but it was not published until 1875. It was later set to music and first appeared as the Advent hymn "In the Bleak Midwinter" in *The English Hymnal* in 1906. The two most famous musical settings for the poem were composed by Gustav Holst and Harold Edwin Darke in the early twentieth century.

The poem is gentle, wise, full of faith, drawing us into mystery, touching the deep longings of the human heart with images that evoke wonder. You will find the poem immediately following this introduction, and you will discover that the headings for each of the forty Advent meditations that follow are successive lines of the poem.

"In the Bleak Midwinter" is about God becoming human, being born in a humble birthplace to a girl, in the midst of heavenly hosts. Midwinter is a season of contrasts, pull, power, and seeming contradiction. Advent has both a severe, cold, wintry feeling and a gentle, warm, summer side.

Feel the cold: "Frosty wind made moan." A sword pierced Mary's heart and she pondered all these things.

Then feel the gentleness, warmth, and humanity: "A breast full of milk / And a manger full of hay." Mary sang: "My soul does magnify the Lord."

The hymn stanzas focus on incarnation, an act full of grace when "heaven cannot hold him." This grace comes to a humble place of human birth, to the humanity of Mary and to our own humanity, in the midst of divine angelic presence. So these meditations focus on the paradox, tension, pull, and contradiction experienced in the coming of Christ from heaven to earth.

The tone of the poem is set by the realities of bleak midwinter. God was born not in the spring or summertime or colorful autumn, but in unwelcoming midwinter. In midwinter, when the cold is not yet over and "Earth stood hard as iron / Water like a stone."

Mary had much to ponder in her heart. She would birth a baby, but no ordinary baby. Gabriel brought her the message, and Mary sang a song. Both message and song speak of the life of this child. The birth did indeed come in "the bleak midwinter" but bore the summer harvest.

The repetition in the first stanza of "in the bleak midwinter" and "snow on snow" is a sign that Advent is always a refrain, repeated and ever in process. I have seen some eighty midwinters, "snow on snow." May these meditations inspire, comfort, and give hope as you experience again the wonder and mystery of Incarnation.

In the peace of the Christ child
Herbert Brokering

In the Bleak Midwinter

by
Christina Georgina Rossetti

In the bleak mid-winter
Frosty wind made moan,
Earth stood hard as iron,
Water like a stone;
Snow had fallen, snow on snow
Snow on snow,
In the bleak mid-winter,
Long ago.

Our God, heaven cannot hold him,
Nor earth sustain;
Heaven and earth shall flee away
When he comes to reign:
In the bleak mid-winter
A stable place sufficed
The Lord God incarnate,
Jesus Christ.

Enough for him, whom Cherubim

Worship night and day,

A breast full of milk

And a manger full of hay;

Enough for him, whom angels

Fall down before,

The ox and ass and camel

which adore.

Angels and archangels

May have gathered there,

Cherubim and seraphim

Thronged the air,

But his mother only,

In her maiden bliss,

Worshipped the Beloved

With a kiss.

What can I give Him,

Poor as I am?

If I were a shepherd

I would bring a lamb,

If I were a wise man

I would do my part,—

Yet what I can I give Him,

Give my heart.

In the bleak midwinter...

God knows when to rebirth earth

In calendars of time

When sun is low when cold has won

When poems look for rhyme

And in the middle of all cold

The warm will soon unfold

WE KNEW WINTER IN THE COUNTRY. I made it come and go by breathing on a cold window pane, creating pictures. Winter drawings decorated the north windows. South windows were colored by frost, winter sun, and fractured light. I still hear myself after seventy-five years: "Mama, come see the winter picture I painted." Papa was the first to leave a warm bed and stoke a banked fire. Papa stirring in the cold country house rings clear to me, the way he wakened us for chores, and the long winter walk to country school. The best window paintings of all were by Jack Frost, who painted all night to amaze us with frosted glass in the morning. I was sure Jack Frost was a disciple of Jesus who only painted winter scenes.

Winter was not a night for a baby to be born outside in a barn, in Nebraska or in Bethlehem. Not even in the warm barn old Pastor Geyer had built for his six horses that we had now for our two cows and winter cats. The wind rattled our tin barn, and there was no stove to warm the hay in Nebraska, or in Bethlehem.

Incarnation is about God in the real world. God in a birth in the cold. God in a barn in a manger bed. God wrapped in a midwinter, a bleak long winter wrapped around a baby, a mother, a people, a nation; God wrapped around cold feet and hands, cold spirits, cold hearts. God among us, all the way into Bethlehem and Minnesota and Pittsburgh and Washington, D.C., and Berlin and Stockholm; God in midwinter. In the middle of winter when the long cold is only half done and the beginning and the end of cold are still far apart. God in the cold with any nation or person or baby when it is way too cold too long. God in the cold. Advent means God is coming in bleak midwinter, when things are far too cold.

Frosty wind made moan...

FROM EARLY CHILDHOOD MY MIND HAS BEEN FILLED WITH THE MOANING OF PRAIRIE WIND. Wind can sing. Wind can make song through reeds and the vibration of strings and beats. The most-played wind ensembles I know are the winds from any direction moaning around eaves and trees facing into a wind. Prairie grass can whistle and make a summer moan. Frosty wind is moaning in another key. *Awesome* is too small a word. Awesome cold winter wind moaning. A fitting word for the season: *awesome*. Listen. Remember.

My mother was a warm woman. Her lap was always ready for us children. My mother moaned. It was more of a wintry moaning. Her hands were sometimes cold, and her head and neck hurt. *Migraine*; we knew the word. Mother moaned as she lay down; I massaged her neck. Her eyes were shut; she knew my child hands. It was a wintry moan. I still hear the moaning of my mother. The touch and the moaning sounds are in me. God came into a moaning world for us all.

God came into a moaning earth. There was and is a moaning too soft and deep to be heard. A moaning still frozen in eaves and rafters and treetops waiting for the one wind and breath that will sing the moan.

Earth was in pain, and God came to Bethlehem. There, all earth's moaning could be heard, and from there a child would touch every moaning mother and father in Judea and the uttermost parts of the earth.

My mother hurt when the seasons were too full. I wanted her to be well for Christmas Eve and birthdays and every morning. So God came to all moaning nations and heard them, knew their voice, felt their moan, touched them, and heard each moaning word. I knew the meaning of my mother's moaning word was "Amen." I did not mention it for fear I was wrong. The moaning refrain was surely: Amen. Amen. Amen. So be it. Truly, truly. Yes.

Wind is breath, life, and spirit

God knows the wintry moan

God hears the sigh of nations

Of moanings all alone

Wind is breath, want, and passion

God knows the moan so still

That hides inside the silence

And lives inside the will

Wind is breath, hope, salvation

God knows our moaning when

Inside the hurt and wanting

God hears the word: Amen

Earth stood hard as iron . . .

EARTH IS SOFT. Now the song: "Earth stood hard as iron."
Earth is soft. I know the earth as a bed of green in spring and
soft beneath September leaves. Now the song: "Earth stood
hard." Earth stands? Earth in winter has no warm lap; earth has
no soft mother's breast. Earth is cold deep down. Winter earth,
cold sometimes seven feet deep, deeper than a grave, hard as iron,
standing. Upright, solid in midwinter. Such a world is a different
world, a hard world. Into this world, God comes.

We have felt this iron underfoot. I watched farmers dig
through this iron to create winter graves. My brother's grave was
in this iron earth. How hard the Kuhlman boy dug to make his a
friend a winter place. I was little and watched. Years later I heard
a North Dakota boy look into his father's wintry tomb and shout:
"Is it cold in there?" He shivered; I put my robe around him.

We wrapped the urn containing my wife's ashes in a homemade blanket made by the grandchildren. The grave seemed
warmer with a blanket. Their young souls felt the warmth.

Hearts can be hard as iron. Hearts can be too cold for seed
and can be too silent. I have known hearts that stood as iron and
lost their warm beat. Mine has done so. I heard a man curse his
best friend and hurry out to take his friend's life. How awful it

must feel to have such a heart in you. God came to warm these places on earth.

Bethlehem was not a safe place. A shed is warm but not warm enough for a newborn. Earth always needs warming so we can lie on the grass and walk barefoot. Earth needs a warm safe place where seed can wake and rise and where ground can green. Earth needs at least a cave with straw and a warm mother and father and a tiny fire or blanket. A people cannot be safe in a place that stands hard as iron.

God, I know the cold
That turns a heart and mind
Too hard for winter breath
Just right for sudden death
In me and humankind.

How deep you warm your earth
With life and summer sun
As in the stable straw
While angels sing hurrah
You send us Christ, your son

Water like a stone...

SO DEEP THE COLD: "WATER LIKE A STONE." Nights could be so cold that we did not let a bucket stay full of water. The water became stone and cracked a seam in the pail. Water can create sculpted castles and forests in wintry art galleries. Rooftops poured ice cones ten feet to the ground; we marveled and licked them.

He was eighteen and climbed a winter willow tree. The trunk was filled with water like a stone. Brittle, fragile, careful. O how we loved this brother. One limb, one break, one fall, a creek below with water like a stone. Heaven. Water like a stone has its own winter rules. These rules are laws that must be obeyed.

I remember haylofts where large chunks of ice were hidden in straw. Water was like stone, and farmers would cut or chip what they needed for iceboxes. On Sundays, we liked chunks of water like stone, a gunny sack; smashing creek ice for a hand-turned freezer gave us winter ice cream. Water like stone was our Sunday dessert.

A son and I went to the funeral home to see her and touch her after the auto accident. She was like a stone. A warm woman like a marble stone. God came to Minnesota to be with the father and son touching a woman cold as a stone. The son screamed: "This is not my mother." He let her go. Death can be more frightening than a water tank freezing to the bottom. Both are very still. Incarnation is about God coming to save the one who no longer feels like your mother or child. Where life is still, too silent, and there is no word or breath or warmth. God is there; we know God knows. God is as silent as we. God, you are not afraid of the silent cold when water turns to stone.

A sword like cold stone pierced Mary's heart.

One breath and God warms what is too cold
God takes the old
God makes old new
God hears the winter moan
Turns what feels like marble stone
To spirits humming in the winter storm
On fire and feeling very warm

Snow had fallen ...

SNOW IS WARMER THAN STONE. Snow can blanket cold and be warm enough to play in for hours. Remember? We faced the sky and our tongues caught flake after flake. Do you remember nibbling on snow balls? A cold season can be friendly. Midwinter can be just right. Hear children crying: "Snow! Snow! O look, snow!"

Christmas cards need some printed falling snow. Falling snow is medicine; falling snow is a blessing. How many times, age after age, the world has taken time out to stand at windows and doorways and watch falling snow.

I wish that once all earth could have a warm dusting of snow and that this could be a sign of one blanket in the universe, and that all earth could hear one carol sung by one choir.

The song sings: "Snow had fallen." What happens after snow has fallen? Birds come out to greet the sun and a white land-scape. Birds look brighter; their colors like the white curtain and blanket. Rabbits come from hiding places and mark new tracks. Rusted iron piles and rubbish heaps pose as pure sculpture. For a while, fallen snow redeems. All beauty is blended.

Why does falling snow seem so friendly? Neighbors step out and meet at doorsteps to talk across fences and alleys about beauty and white and clean, and their voices are kind. If snow fell in Bethlehem, surely Joseph went to the door and said: "Look, Mary, the earth is pure white." And Mary said: "Of course, Joseph. The child. Remember what Gabriel said." And Mary held Jesus and showed the baby how snow had fallen.

> *God's snow has fallen. What do I see?*
>
> *The dancing flakes, hilarity*
>
> *Wonder, grace, and charity*
>
> *God's snow has fallen. What do I hear?*
>
> *Snow bird and silent deer*
>
> *A hearty bird, a chirp, a cheer*
>
> *God's snow has fallen. What do I pray?*
>
> *A joy too great to sing or say*
>
> *That God make glad my heart today*

Snow on snow . . .

"SNOW, SNOW," WE CHILDREN SHOUTED. Mother baked cookies; Father sang. Father played piano and our house sang with cookie aroma. Father sang and helped us feel the creek rise, the water table fill, and the moisture store for summer harvest.

God comes in the snow and father sings. The child in the manger sleeps. He will be named the Bread of Life. The child will be called the Water of Life. The child will lift a cup and say: "It snowed in winter. The vineyard yielded a harvest. Rain for the just and the unjust. Take and drink." Father sings the Gloria.

Snow on snow! All morning, noon, chore time, nightfall, through the night, and the morning waking call: "It's still snowing." How warm it looks, a white blanket. In the eyes of a child, angel feathers, warm as down, complete peace, the world at rest. Come, Holy Spirit, descend on us we pray.

O see the snow, the inches grow. The fence is covered. Peace on earth. Everything so white and warm.

O the beauty of the white sculpted evergreen. Branches weigh heavy, but they will not break. Do not shake the branches; they know how to bear their weight. Watch the trees and see how they carry a burden. Be not afraid of "snow on snow."

O the pure white shapes of rusted cars and dead hedges and trash cans and tin sheds and abandoned houses, one white landscape. Look! Look! I see. I see. Earth decorated for a while to look like castles and cathedrals. I see the glory of incarnation. God is on earth, and Immanuel is here. *Incarnation*: a word full of beauty. Earth and we are in a quiet white crèche.

Snow on snow. Deep enough to hide and warm iron earth. Fallen snow of God upon the ground. If not snow then rain and sun and light and peace upon the earth. God comes like snow on snow.

You come like ocean waves and touch the shore
Again, again, once more, once more
Incarnate life like snow on snow
You come and leave, you stay, you go
We wait, you come like snow on snow

In the bleak midwinter ...

ANOTHER BLEAK MIDWINTER. Then another and another. Another winter with earth standing like iron and water like stone. Another saint en route to God: quiet, cold, a neighbor, a grandparent very still, Alzheimer's, cancer, bankrupt. Bleak winters come and go in many styles. Some midwinters are not soon done, some not nearly finished for a long, long winter time. In my eighty years there have been more than eighty bleak midwinters. And always the thaw and high sun and trickle of a creek in the woods. And Easter.

Incarnation is never over. God in midwinter is a continual visitor, present again and again. Knock, knock! Who's there? I Am.

Winter after winter and the next one ready to come from the north. It's very cold! Help. Then the promise of God: I know. I am here. I know the cold. I know the deep frost. I feel the cold feet and fingertips. I have walked the iron earth. I hear the silence in the garden, in Eden, and in the cemetery. I know the cold winters that blow into your life. I know, I know, and I see the snow on snow.

It is cold outside, and the trees tremble. It is sometimes colder inside where minds and hearts are set to freeze. They are in another bleak midwinter, and another. And God said: My people's hearts are sometimes cold. I will come to bathe your feet and warm you from head to toe. I will warm you from inside out. Take and eat; take and drink. Again, again, eat and drink. It is only midwinter; wait.

Why are you sobbing? Cry, louder if you must. It is only midwinter. Cry out: "Enough!" When the dark is too long and the earth feels like iron, cry: "My God, my God."

Incarnation allows us to holler: Help.

O God, we come, we come
Weak and cold and on the run
The world once new seems oh so old
And kingdoms' warm now far too cold
One bleak midwinter, and then one more
Ah, peace on earth, then one more war
Ah, peace on earth and war no more

Long ago.

LONG AGO. LONG, LONG AGO. Before all time, God comes into the earth. God comes inside the earth, above, around, beneath, within, to the earth. Listen: "I knew when the morning star began. I knew you from the beginning." As a child I already believed that I was always on God's mind.

God said: "Let there be light." And there is light. The same light as from the beginning. God said: "Where are you in the garden?" And we still say, "Here we are, hiding under the snow cover, for we are ashamed." The baby in the barn will melt the cold and reopen the garden gate.

God said: "Here I am. It is I. Be not afraid. Only believe." The words of God have never quit. Listen, and hear the words of long ago. "Be not afraid; only believe." The psalms still sing the words. Prophets still echo the promise. Babes still proclaim the trust.

Go back to long ago, to markers on the tombstones and to names of saints and verses always true and carved in marble. Go back to hymns of family and to refrains of mothers humming prayers upon infant faces. Go back to parent adoration and all the ways to keep the baby in the barn alive and warm. Long ago, when prayers began and are never outgrown and close a day as they did in your own bed long ago: believing, believing. Go back to long ago and find the roots that still feed you and the flow that reaches into rivers of life that fed your world, of long ago.

Go back to blessings that still bless as they blessed ten thousand years before. Incarnation begun has never quit. Heaven has always been on earth. Earth knows God.

I believed more when the Heckels came to visit our parsonage. They were old, from long ago. Now it is my turn to be old, from long ago, so that some might believe more.

Long ago you made the sun
All of life was then begun
You knew of me, you knew my name
Wrapped good gifts for when I came
That was 'fore long, long ago
And eons, eons in a row
When you first made eternity
You said my name, you knew of me

Our God,
heaven cannot hold him . . .

HOW BIG IS HEAVEN? Will all the saints and the saved fit?
Will there be room in heaven for everyone forever and ever?
What little believer has not wondered about the size of heaven?

Now a more amazing picture: Heaven cannot hold an infant.
"Heaven cannot hold him." A new thought for the child alive
in me. If we sing, "Come into my heart, Lord Jesus," why can't
heaven hold him? Did the Christ want to come to fill the earth?
He came to Nazareth, to a woman, and then rode on a donkey
to Bethlehem. He took the bumpy ride, the discomfort, the
excitement of a new mother who pondered in her heart while
the Word rode to a stable to be born. Heaven cannot hold him;
heaven gave him to earth.

God, why did you send the Word to dwell among us? Did
he ask to come? Did he know what this could mean? Did you
warn him about the garden, and the stone, and the swords and
lanterns, when he would sweat blood and kneeling learn to say:
"I will"? Was it his will to come to earth?

Sometimes I believe he had to come. Heaven was too small;
the grace of heaven was overflowing. Heaven had the key to
Eden, and he came to open the garden gate. This was his work.

Some call him Immanuel, some Messiah, and some name him Adam. Eden is not gone. Eden has a new gate, and the child holds the key.

Adam wants back into the garden. Adam is looking for the tree. Eve is looking for her children. Heaven will open the garden that is shut. The child will do it. The child has the key to the garden of grace, the garden of God. Look! I believe. The child holds the key; heaven cannot hold him.

My God, my God, how can this be
That heaven and eternity
Are full of grace, so full of love
That Christ did come from far above
And bring the gift of your Amen
In choirs and child to Bethlehem?
And since Messiah holds the key
Unlock your garden deep in me

Nor earth sustain . . .

WHAT A THOUGHT BY THE SONGWRITER. "Heaven cannot hold him." And now a counter-thought: "Nor earth sustain" him. Heaven is too full, overflowing, but earth is too empty and cannot keep him alive. Such contrasts tell a story beyond understanding. These two thoughts turn truth into wonder. Be amazed with me at these two pictures. The Christ torn because heaven cannot hold him and yet earth cannot sustain him. This is a season of wonderment, contrasts, mystery, and faith. It is a time to feel the torn world.

He came from heaven to earth, to Bethlehem, a gift from heaven. And earth sent him back to heaven from Calvary. Was the Christ so bright and right and good we could not comprehend or grasp him? Do we vacillate with Pilate so that we do not know what to do with him?

He came to reopen paradise. Paradise is the garden of human birth. It was closed and an angel came to guard it. The garden became a grave. Now Messiah, the baby, came to live, die, be laid in a garden, a grave, and be raised. What is this second garden? The garden of human rebirth! The angels are no longer closing the entrance. Read the gospels: They stand at the entrance, opening the tomb, declaring: "He is not here; he is risen and goes before you."

That is why the baby in Bethlehem came. To bring the key to unlock the garden, to unlock the grave, and to waken from death. Earth cannot sustain him. Earth flogged him and crucified him. This season is about a God who goes where we are flogged, despised, betrayed, denied, and killed. For this reason, God came to Bethlehem, to hear Rachel weep and to hear the feet of Herod's soldiers and angels marching in Berlin and Salem and Korea and Columbia. The boots of Herod's army still walk the earth and make the babies of Bethlehem cry and mothers weep.

The good news? The door to paradise is now open. Death, you have no more sting.

Dearest Jesus, little one
Come as stranger, sister, son
Gift of heaven, Light of light
Angels' music, God's delight
Heaven in a woman's womb
Born to open wide the tomb
Keep for me the golden key
To unlock eternity

Heaven and earth
shall flee away . . .

SHEPHERDS AND KINGS CAME. All hurried to kneel and worship. Hurry, God is on earth, in the hay, in a town, with people, with us. Immanuel means God is with us. God is asleep; the Prince of Peace sleeps in Mary's lap. God is with us as an infant.

God lives, grows in stature. God lives, suffers, is crucified, risen, ascended. God walks the human way, our way. This is the way that goes all the way to the grave and to glory. He ascends and is at the right hand of the Father. From there he will come again.

The child will return. The child who was at Mary's breast is at the right hand of God. The one in the manger is on the throne, and he will come again. Heaven cannot hold him. Heaven and earth shall flee away.

O the glory when he came to Bethlehem. Glory filled the skies, and all angels sang at once. The heavens were ablaze, and earth was dumbfounded. We still make bright lights, and choirs rehearse nonstop. We now glorify! Jesus came to Mary and was born in secret in a cave, one child born in all the world, and he will come again.

He will come again in a cloud and the holy angels with him, in bright glory and with trumpet sounds and with sight and light so great, so brilliant, so blinding, so glorious that earth will flee away, and heaven too. "Heaven and earth shall flee away."

Jesus Christ is too big for heaven and for earth. Heaven and earth will flee and be made new.

Where do they flee? I do not know. How do they flee? I do not know. Why do they flee? He will open a new earth and a new heaven. Is this the reopening of Paradise? Is this heaven and earth become one? He will make a new beginning. The Word will say: "Let there be a new creation," and it will be so.

Heaven and earth shall flee away
And then the great surprise!
All things made new
And glory the surprise

Heaven and earth shall flee away
And God at human breast
Then life and death , the open grave
The cloud, God's peace and rest

When he comes to reign . . .

WHEN WILL ALL THIS HAPPEN? When will there be a new heaven and a new earth? When he comes to reign! In glory!

In the beginning God made. When he comes to reign, God will begin a new beginning. God will say and there will be. Will there be light and sky and water and trees and birds and creeping things and fish, and will it be very good? We will see. So it began. And when Christ comes to reign, heaven and earth will flee. We have not yet seen, nor have our ears heard, of such creation. My friend Emma says, "We ain't seen nothin' yet."

And God will say, "Very good," and it will be so. In the twinkling of an eye: changed, new, glory.

From where will God reign? How does God reign now? From above, from within, from the heart, through the bread, in the neighbor, by grace, from beyond, by forgiveness, through the water, by the word. How will God reign? By grace; God is grace. By love; God is love. By life; God is life.

Who could have dreamed of the years given on earth? Who could have planned a universe and people from generation to generation? Who could have brought so many to bow and kneel by a manger in Bethlehem? How can one word, *love*, be the one law for all humankind? How will God reign? Through love.

Will the reign have choirs? At least. Will there be vistas and awesome sunsets? At least. Will there be joy and laughter? At least. How will the new reign be? A new time, a new space, a new heaven, a new earth, a new Bethlehem, a new Calvary, a new garden. New. Everything made new.

When? Today. When? Tomorrow.

When? When he comes to reign.

Jesus. Jesus, when you come again
When you come to reign in glory
Will it be the old, old story
Or a new one you will tell
Beside the one we know so well?
Ah the wonder we will see
Inside your eternity!

In the bleak midwinter . . .

Remember, O remember

Bleak midwinters came in December

Some in the summer, or in September

Remember, I remember

O GOD, I HAVE HAD BLEAK MIDWINTERS; THREE ALREADY.
Will there be more? Last year at this time. Remember? No more
work. Three months ago. Remember? Death in the family. Last
month. Remember? Stillborn. God, I had my bleak midwinter.
Are there more?

God, I remember. There was the winter wedding. A family
reunion. The surprise visit of an old relative. A healing we never
expected. All in a bleak midwinter.

The sudden storm. Five hundred sheep frozen on a ranch. Is
that a bleak midwinter? Where is the cave, the shed, the bed, the
hay, the manger? Another midwinter and another and another.
Soon the next, and then the next.

Winter after winter, prophets keep promising, mothers and
Rachel keep weeping, Hannah keeps praising, Herod's soldiers
keep trampling new meadows and hot deserts to hunt Rachel's
children. While children carol in falling snow, enemies plant land

mines like tulips near swings and playgrounds. Infants are held hostage, and the child in the hay has no swaddling clothes. The poor hide their faces to beg in silence and will never know the joy of firstfruits and a tithe.

One midwinter prepares for the next. When one has found the secret inside a bleak winter, one is ready for the next. There is more than one midwinter, and they are not all in December.

> *O Lord, another bleak midwinter*
> *They come, they go like snow on snow*
> *Some are full of joy and peace*
> *Some are long and cold that will not cease*
> *Some are fear and tears and Rachel's cry*
> *Some come to wrap us when we die*
> *Oh bleak midwinter be Thou my friend*
> *And hold me warm when comes the end*

A stable place sufficed ...

IF I WERE THE LORD GOD, I TOO WOULD HAVE PREPARED THE STABLE PLACE FOR IMMANUEL. Because I was a country boy, the stable place was my favorite room, with fresh hay for the cows and clean golden straw for the bed. How deep my father piled the straw in the barn Christmas Eve. I wished to sleep there also, the Christ child and me in the same hay. The stable place sufficed for me then.

Now I know more about infant mortality and the treasure and protection our children received at birth time. As a father, I did not choose a stable birth. Yet, a stable birth would be welcomed by millions of parents on earth. If my father had a birthing barn with golden straw twelve inches thick, mothers and fathers would stand in line for their child's birth. This is where God came to be born, in a predicted and yet unlikely place. Only believers knew that Bethlehem and a stable was the place.

A stable sufficed for the Christ; Jesus, Immanuel, the Messiah born and hardly any noticeable preparation. No announcement cards sent out, no doctors appointment, no prenatal checkups, no trained gynecologist. No room in the inn and no handmaid and no mama in the room. Just Joseph and whatever donkeys or camels or sheep housed in the stable place that night.

Whatever was there, as usual, sufficed. The birth came into an ordinary place.

Dr. Luke, who must have wished to be personally present, records: "He went to be registered with Mary. . . . While they were there . . . she gave birth." Anna, Mary's mother, must have made sure that what Mary would need was in a special bag. That was all she sent as she waved goodbye to her teenage daughter.

No castle inside a safe moat. No palace with a mother queen. No home of a high priest with fine silk curtains. No baby hospital. No Mayo Clinic or reserved birthing room in Jerusalem. A stable place sufficed. A stable was where God needed to come. A very ordinary, out of the way place.

> *Infant Jesus came to earth*
> *Human mother, human birth*
> *On the ground where all began*
> *Donkey, doves, the hay, the lamb*
> *Stars and straw above, around*
> *Shepherd smells and angel sound*
> *God has blessed the common place*
> *The ordinary filled with grace*

The Lord God incarnate . . .

The Word became flesh and slept in the hay
Saw where we are and walked the same way
Born of a girl, born of a womb
Climbed a high hill, awoke in a tomb
Though the Messiah, the Counselor, Lord
Found life in a mother's umbilical cord

GOD INCARNATE. This is the miracle, mystery, the wonder of this season. The Lord God in the girl, as a newborn, sleeping in the hay, human. What a comfort. The Lord God is like me, in me, to me; "God is with us" was the promise to Mary. His name is God-with-us. So sacred.

Birth is sacred. How mysterious is our own beginning. How miraculous is the birth cry. I was the one asked to cut the umbilical cord. I faced a ruddy-faced grandson struggling to make his first breath and cry. He left the safety of the womb and was now in a world of dust and storm and flood and hunger and music and swings and noise. I played a song on my harmonica and brought him into this world with music in Minneapolis. The angels did the same in Bethlehem. Mine was a simple celebration.

"Love, love, love" on the harmonica. No angel choirs singing or shepherds running with gifts or wise men setting out in a caravan. No one searching stars and sky and manuscripts to prove he was the child all were waiting for. The Lord God, Immanuel, lay in the manger.

God in the child. Only believe. Only wonder, be amazed.

God born of a girl. Be amazed, dazzled, comforted.

God incarnate, sixteen inches long, weighing six pounds and six ounces. Be dumbfounded. Only believe.

God incarnate. God in our nature, with a temperature of 98.6, with veins and arteries, alive, hungry, enjoying a glass of wine, thirsty. God incarnate.

God near; God here. God knows. Ah, the peace that passes understanding.

God, do not explain to me
The full meaning of your love and grace
And the wonder in a holy time and space

Jesus Christ.

Two realms, blended, heaven and earth
In one stable and in one birth

JESUS, THE HUMAN ONE. Christ, the holy one. God and man. God came all the way, all the way into human form, as we are! When we speak the name "Jesus Christ," we say heaven and earth, human and divine.

Jesus Christ. What does this mean?

Jesus, Mary's baby, and Christ, God's own son. To me this means the one on Mary's lap, Jesus, is at the right hand of God, Christ; what a wide angle picture of the child, from earth to heaven and heaven to earth. One long lineage; one long promise, hope and salvation. From the hay to the throne and everything between. This is God's gift of grace to us. God has gone every step of that way, and it is our way. We do not travel from womb to throne alone. I do not travel from Beatrice, Nebraska, to heaven alone.

This one, "Jesus Christ," who came is coming with choirs and horns and fanfare in the sky. Many hear the coming with grand chorales. In New Orleans they will hear the coming again as jazz, and in Nashville perhaps as the best country music. In Berlin they will hear the coming as a symphony.

He is coming soon. That is what was said all through the centuries of prophets, priests, and kings. Be ready, he is coming soon. Stay hopeful. When I was eight we heard my brother sing "Lost in the Night" in the Hebron College choir. I will not forget the Russian Orthodox chant throughout: "Hospodi pomilui" (Lord, have mercy). I will always feel the comfort of the mantra, "He is coming soon. He is coming soon. He is coming soon." For me, soon meant "for sure."

In the Holy Communion liturgy we say all this as we come forward to eat and to drink: "He has come, Christ is here, Christ will come again."

Ah the wonder when we blend three times
What was and is and will be
And in the wedding of these three
We find the nearness of eternity
In the Kyrie Hospodi pomilui

Enough for him,
whom Cherubim ...

THE STABLE, STRAW, MARY'S BREAST, AND CHERUBIM
WERE ENOUGH FOR HIM. Enough. Not too little, but enough. No
complaints. No calling the health department or the front desk
for more service; no demanding clean sheets and a midwife. The
stable was enough.

Breath of donkeys, sheep, and camels will warm the air. My
cow in midwinter warmed the air in the little barn my father
had built. The body temperature of a beast in a stable can help
warm a baby. Dogs have kept trapped skiers from freezing. A donkey and a sheep can make a difference. The stable was enough.

Joseph had a coat. Mary had a shawl. Together they could
warm a place for the child in the hay. The child could sleep
between them. We have all huddled in the cold and warmed each
other. In our country church, a cold pew, the pump organ, and
father preaching were enough. When still too cold we sat close
with blankets over our laps. It was primitive, and it was enough.
How many are born each day with little comfort and protection;
they have enough. When there is no more to have, many soon
know they have enough. Jesus had the hay and donkey, Mary's
shawl and breast, and Joseph's coat.

In my early ministry I often guided young people to unforgettable experiences. Several times we celebrated Christmas in a garage, for the stable of the inn was a garage for beasts of burden. I hid New Testaments in a hayloft, and we found Luke 2 and read the story while sitting in straw. God in the hay is beyond imagination, so we imagined and believed.

God is a God of abundance. See what God spent on his own Son. There was no private birthing room for the family. The cave was enough. See the wardrobe. There was no baby shower. Swaddling clothes were enough. The God of abundance did not lavish attention on his own dear son. There is enough for all newborns. See the child in Bethlehem asleep. He had enough. There is always enough when we know what is enough.

Jesus, your wardrobe was so very small
A knapsack, dream, some hay and drink
Very small that is all. Enough, that is all

Worship night and day . . .

Shhh. By faith we hear a heaven sound
Angel hymns upon the ground
By faith we hear them any time
As song in harmony and rhyme

CHERUBIM WORSHIP THE CHILD DAY AND NIGHT. In worship, do you hear the white sound of their singing? They kneel, and the manger is surrounded by holiness. Holiness is God's light, and light makes warm. If angels are blessing, then their breath will warm the room. If they hold infants, as angels do, those newborns will feel the comfort. I only begin to know what cherubim do for a child they worship.

Cherubim tend us day and night. Whatever God came to Bethlehem to bring I will take as a gift. I will ask no questions but only give thanks. Angels bring worship by their mere presence.

When little, I learned an old prayer I still pray in the dark. In the old German prayer, angels surround my bed and protect me with weapons gilded with gold. Night after night I was kept safe in my upstairs bedroom. In cold subzero winters and in the warm silent summer dark, I was protected. There was never a battle around my bed. Who would war against a circle of cherubim? We sang the old prayer of Paul Gerhardt: "Breit aus die Pflügel Beide" ("Spread wide your wings"). The hymn was our battle cry in the night. No enemy could penetrate the cherubim and our singing.

In Bethlehem, I noticed Orthodox priests worshipping when no parish members were present. Their house of prayer was a few feet from the nativity site. How did they worship without the people? I heard the answer. Heaven is always in worship, night and day. What the priests do is tune into heaven's liturgy at any time. Heaven with seraphim and cherubim lead the universe in worship. Creation is called to worship at all times, night and day.

> *When spirits battle in my room*
> *And fill my soul with gloom*
> *I call on Cherubim in flight*
> *To come by day or come by night*
> *With songs and candlelight*

breast full of milk . . .

IMAGINE, GOD AT A MOTHER'S BREAST. Jesus at Mary's breast full of milk. A sacred picture of "Give us this day our daily bread." A child at mother's breast like someone taking Eucharist. What more is there? This milk is life to the child, as bread and wine are to us. Often I have wondered if this is in fact their first communion. See their eyes and fingers grappling the full breast of milk. I saw it often in our country church as mothers of infants moved close to the steel stove and nursed their children. On the holy day of communion I marveled while mothers nursed and the adults went forward to drink of the one cup. I thought of all mothers' milk as one drink for all babies. I still think this way.

"A breast full of milk" has been painted by many master painters. El Greco's *The Holy Family* is a beautiful portrait of the Virgin Mary breastfeeding. The child is reaching to grab his mother's hand. Her breast is serving him well. He has only to take and drink. Mary is like the new Eve, unashamed of her body as she was before the Fall.

There are many pictures and paintings of grace. Is Jesus at a breast full of milk not a picture of grace? Is not every infant nursing at a mother's breast a sign of grace? All the child does is receive the milk, take, and drink. The child must receive it, must drink to benefit. Grace does not force itself on us. Grace is there for us to embrace and take and impart. Grace is nourishment, nurturing, satisfying, healing, and sacramental.

When our children nursed there was rocking, humming, stillness, peacefulness, contentment in the whole house. I did not try to understand; the spirit was holy. The whole world was satisfied, as was I. In the common stable, as in all places with just enough, there is a peace that passes understanding. I do not wish to comprehend the great meaning of Jesus Christ and a breast full of milk.

> *Early life begins as sacrament*
> *Take and eat; take and drink*
> *Which causes me to wonder and to think*
> *That Mary knew, and Joseph too*
> *That holding Christ where ere they went*
> *They held for us the sacrament*

And a manger full of hay ...

Tiny things like smells of cows and Christmas straw
Fill my mind with awe

GOD, YOU KNOW MY FEELINGS ABOUT HAY IN A BARN AT
CHRISTMAS. Childhood seems never to pass away. I still smell
the deep fresh straw on the barn floor and the good hay in the
manger for the cow. It is a refrain of mine. We had one cow, and
each year she was a Christmas cow. Sometimes she calved, and as
we entered the little barn we heard the mother softly mooing to
her baby. She wanted to know where her baby was and to protect
it with her life. Mary must have felt the same. My cow was in
a familiar stable and knew me. Mary was in a foreign place, but
Joseph was near. And the promise and presence of Gabriel never
left her.

What did Mary sing in the stable? I imagine she often sang
the Magnificat, and Joseph listened to the words. She had learned
to sing her faith in the synagogue or from her mother. She knew
the tunes. Mary was a girl and may have known some of her own
country music.

We do not know who may have come to visit in the inn and celebrate the birth. We know so little of what we pretend to know. We decorate the manger full of hay with color, paintings, and poetry.

Today it is not possible to find the hay in the stable. The little room in Bethlehem is full of honor and glory and majesty and worship and reverence. Candles from the world and lanterns of many kinds cover what was once stable and hay. The room is layered with love and flooded with reverence from every age.

If there was hay to be seen two thousand years ago, it is now scattered into the homes of pilgrims who have visited the stable site. If I had seen straw I would have taken just one piece for a bookmark. Just one straw. Souvenirs take us back to holy sites.

O God, where is the hay?
Is there nothing left of that first Christmas day
Except a glow too great for a tiny cave?
Where is the halo and the afterglow
On fire in all who come to bow
And feel the birth is here and now?
O God, where is the hay?
And where is the star that came so far?

Enough for him, whom angels ...

Eighty years and so much stuff
Teach me Lord: Enough is enough!

HOW CAN SO LITTLE BE ENOUGH? Little was enough for
the child.

God is a God of minimalism. Seven loaves and three fish
fed five thousand. How? God has a secret of stewardship. God
breaks things open, and there is more and more inside. We find
this in planting an ear of corn. One ear of corn will grow a field.
For planting, we cut a potato in several pieces so each has an eye.
One potato could grow five hills of potatoes. Enough is a matter
of dividing.

Holy Communion is about dividing. Not eating a loaf
alone. Blessing and breaking it and eating it with others. We
know this by wearing hand-me-downs. Wearing the clothes of
an older sibling was sometimes an honor; I felt very close to them.

The stable was enough for him. He had come from realms
of glory. Christ was the Word, who said, "Let there be light," and
there was light. Now he lay inside a dark stable near an oil lamp
lit by Joseph. In the beginning he said, "Let there be the birds of

the air," and now a few found their way into the warmth of the cave to roost, sing, and sleep.

With one word he had made the universe, and now he lay in straw, having just premiered a birth cry. His word woke stars and eons, and now he clung to Mary's breast for a drink. Without the girl he could not live. Without Joseph's dream he would be trampled by the wrath of Herod's army.

The stable is enough for him. Hand carved nativity sets cost more than Joseph and Mary spent with their firstborn in Bethlehem. With one El Greco, Jesus could have bought the hotels of Bethlehem and all of the Holy Land. Read what he had in Luke 2; it was enough.

God, you look from deep inside
Where more and more, still more does hide
You take a crumb and you unfold
We eat, we see and we behold
You take a simple kneeling place
Unwrap for us your gifts of grace
One ear of corn can grow a field
What is the measure Christ does yield?

Fall down before . . .

GOD, YOUR ANGELS FALL DOWN BEFORE THE INFANT, FOR
THIS IS TRUE WORSHIP. Nothing in return; a complete offering. Complete adoration through which the babe sleeps; their
petitions hear no response. Angels fall down; the baby sleeps.
Their singing receives no applause. The baby is nursing from
Mary. Their bowing does not catch his eye. His eyelids are tired,
drooping, resting; he is half awake, soon to be fast asleep in the
way of babies. The countenance of angels shows high praise. The
child's eyes face the mother only; she has the child's full attention.
Angels fall down before him; he is with Mary, no wonder he is at
peace. Angels adore.

Why would not angels fall down, worship, and be amazed?
Angels know the Word as it is in heaven; now they see the Word
as it is on earth. The Word has become flesh and dwells on earth.
What a contrast, paradox, contradiction: the Word that created all
things being fed, diapered, and kept alive by mother's milk. With
the angels, we face God's dumbfounding mystery. The miracle
of this birth is meant not to be comprehended but to save. Awe
is the prelude to believing. Wonder wakens trust. Mystery opens
the window to holiness. Angels fall down in worship; they are the
offering to the child.

Years ago, Mr. Benjamin in San Antonio wanted to worship Christ in a church drama. He asked me how he should kneel. I asked him to show me. As when he was a child in England, he surrendered himself completely. This was his only rehearsal. I did not show him; he knew.

In the last years of the Christ child's life, angels often appeared. They did not fall down. They sat and stood and appeared and announced. How different in the song "In the Bleak Midwinter." In the song they fell down, prostrate, faces to the earth. I have prostrated myself in the Holy Land. I once bowed down and lay prostrate on a flat stone, the stone where it was reported that Jesus' body lay to prepare for his burial. It was a new, holy act of worship for me. Sometimes I roll over in bed and lay prostrate before the child. I will do so often this season.

God, I have seen worshippers fall down to worship Thee
Their faces on mother earth; it is their charity
No longer can I bow low, or kneel
Yet all that angels feel I too do feel
To give my body, spirit, all
And lay it in the cattle stall
As humble, total offering
While choirs sing

The ox and ass and camel . . .

A garage or abandoned car
Is no place for newborns to sleep
Unless there is no other place as bed
To lay their head

THE OX AND ASS AND CAMEL WERE THE CHILD'S TRANSPOR-
TATION FROM ONE PLACE TO ANOTHER. God of gods and Light of
light in a mother, on a donkey, in a dark room with camel and ass
and ox. They traveled from Nazareth, not at the speed of light or by
monorail, but to the trot of a donkey. The one who said, "Let there
be light," asleep near an ox in the night. Speed of light and speed of
ox side by side.

For years we drove secondhand cars. They were what we
could afford. I would look closely for rust, feel oil coming from the
exhaust, and pray the price was right. My salary did not allow us to
drive what others drove. When something needed repair, my son
and I would hunt through acres of dumped cars and find the part
to install. We were not embarrassed by a rusted fender. God was not
ashamed to be transported by donkey and ox. God came poor.

Do the poor finally learn not to be embarrassed or ashamed? I
have seen poor people camping by the thousands along runways at

airfields. It is home. The aroma of burnt fuel is their night air. Do they know the story of the Holy One, who came to sleep in hay?

In Mexico, before the main door of a great cathedral, were large cardboard boxes with many families sound asleep inside them. Not in a manger, but in an empty cardboard box. Perhaps they knew the story often read in the cathedral, the story of God in the hay in the box. Under tin can lean-tos in Manila beside four-star hotels, we saw families having meals as though by candlelight. They were in their own stable and inn where God came to bless the poor. In Idaho, we saw Native Americans sleeping in vacant cars, one a blue rusted convertible. They slept under the big blue sky.

The poor found their tin shed, rusted car, cardboard box, or runway. It was their resting place near ox, ass, and camel. A very humble place can be home.

God, I saw you near the runway in Delhi
And in a cardboard box in Mexico
While myriad angels watch did keep
It sounded like you were fast asleep
And when the straw is all you have for a bed
What is the pillow that you use beneath your head?

Ox and ass and camel adore.

All nature sings!

The stars, the cat, the lamb

Each saying in a different tune

Here I am—Here I am

All nature sings!

The oak, the bloom, the seed

Sometimes the song of summer

Sometimes the broken reed

I FEEL ADORATION IN FORESTS AS TREES GREEN, PRAISE WITH FRUIT, AND SHOW REVERENCE IN AUTUMN COLOR. In midwinter, trees laced in snow stand like candles side by side. Their winter limbs bow in adoration. I see it, for it is in the eye of the beholder.

As a child, the wooden animals carved in Bavaria made the crèche most sacred to me. When we unwrapped the ox and the donkey to set them facing the child, the Christ child seemed to grow even more special. We expected Mary and Joseph and shepherds to adore; with the ox near the manger, my child eyes could see the universe bowing before him. Not just shepherds, but all creation.

In my imagination, this opened the stable to goats and dogs and cats, which easily show devotion. My dogs, Skippy and Peggy Ann, were present at the crèche. They looked on from a distance and seemed more devoted to me than to the Christ in the manger. When I held them beside the crèche, they, with me, adored. One does not like to adore alone. In this season, the universe adores.

There needs to be a time for ox and donkey, sheep and stars to be called to worship. Artists and poets have long included nature in the congregation's worship. They have been carved in altars and pews, set into cathedral windows, and etched in bronze bells. Mathew, Mark, Luke, and John are symbolized by animals and birds. What church does not know the lamb and dove? O God, all nature sings; it is true.

Just once to see all nature and universe sing praise
And hear a tune to God when weeping willow sways
I wish each single cedar in wood or mountain side
Would sing with owls and beaver and dens where coyotes hide
I wish a wooden donkey and plastic manger scene
Could make one sound for Christmas to make the air serene

Angels and archangels
May have gathered there . . .

What angels in heaven would not wish to stay
To see the Lord God sound asleep in hay?
What angels in heaven would not swing low
To see believers come and go?

TO HAVE PRINCES AND PRINCESSES ATTENDING A NEW-
BORN IS MORE THAN ONE WOULD HOPE FOR. But what if kings
and queens were present also? What if presidents and judges were
trained as midwives or nurses to tend mother and child? Oh, to
have them "gathered there." Gathered there with their staff and
servants and singers and medical teams and wise men. What a
royal visitation that would be.

I remember how Bishop Pautke from Lübeck, Germany,
whom we knew through refugee work, arrived in time for the
birth of our second born. He stood before my wife and infant
son with a bouquet hid behind his back. What honor and glory
and royalty he brought to the birth room. There he was with a
smile, fire in his eyes, and a halo on him like an angel or archangel.

So what do archangels bring to the stable? Raphael, who are you? "I am the angel who is the healer, the main physician serving Almighty God. I can summon healers for the child." Michael, who are you? "I protect the earth; I battle Satan." Gabriel, who are you? "I am the messenger of Almighty God who brought the promise directly to Mary. I told her she would be a mother; she said, 'So be it.' Then she sang the Magnificat. I, Gabriel, will keep God's message clear."

How many angels are in the room with the child? Angels fill the stable to the ceiling, ready to serve the child, embroidering every cloud. As a boy I loved sitting on our living room floor at a conference of clergy talking about matters beyond the imagination. My favorite debate year after year was how many angels could stand on the point of a pin. If that many could stand on a pin point, then imagine how many could stand inside the stable ready to serve the child.

> *How good to be served from heaven's side.*
> *Where grace is deep and far and wide*
> *And angels serve from every side*

Cherubim and seraphim . . .

Ah the watchful wings of angels

Warriors shooting darts of love

Medicine now born of heaven

Sent to earth from far above

ANGELS SERVE AND SING; THAT IS HOW I ALWAYS SAW ANGELS. Early in my life, I believed that cherubim served and seraphim sang. Whether true or not, these two words covered all that angels did: they sang, they served. This is an image I have remembered for eighty years. So through the years I have had angels singing and serving. These two words have grown in my mind to cover the ministries of God. Serving and singing have guided me for eighty years.

A cherubim is a many-winged angel, sometimes part animal; they served to pull the chariot of the Almighty. Their overarching wings decorated the temple, and beneath them rested the Ark. They were in the vision of Ezekiel. The divine throne rested on four cherub wings. So they were the guardian spirits for the Ark of the Covenant, the Tree of Life, and of my bed in Nebraska.

A cherub is a small angel portrayed as a child with a chubby, rosy face. So what does this child angel do? They may guard, and with their arrows they shoot sheathes of love. Love is the greatest weapon of angelic warriors; they battle with love.

We all have childhood pictures of angels. In our bedroom we had a picture of angels carrying a child over a bridge to safety. The artist portrayed at least two times in a child's life: angels carrying a child over pain and danger to safety, and angels carrying a child over a river into heaven. They must have been cherubim, God's guardians.

Ah, to hear old hymns of angels
Savored in the mystery of grace
Seraphs, Cherubs singing, serving
Continually the human race

Thronged the air ... ...

THE SPACE OVERHEAD IN THE AIR SEEMS ENDLESS AND
WILL SURELY HOLD A THRONG OF ANGELS. As a child I studied
the air above and around. I did so lying on pasture grass and
looking up and out. In December, I looked out the north window into stars and stars. During Lenten evening services, I often
lay in a pew or on my mother's lap and stared into the vast empty
space overhead to the old tin ceiling. Then I would close my eyes
and look past the ceiling into the night sky outside. I measured
space with imagination. There is room to throng the air. Looking
out and up, there is room.

I have seen migrating geese flying through the air and
known that on the other side of their formation was more space,
endless space. Migrating geese cannot throng the air; there is still
space. I have seen bees swarm and darken the sky like a cloud;
when I saw them all follow the queen to an apple limb, I saw
there were not enough of them to throng the air. Only angels
can throng a space, even the whole air. I never worried that when
they filled the air they might create a traffic jam or huge impasse.
Angels allow us to work through them and not be hampered.

When angels throng the air, I imagine they fill space with energy, spirit, life, light, power, and calm. They glorify the air with light.

Joseph could get in the way, so Mary might say: "Joseph, where you are standing I cannot see the child." If angels were between Mary and the child, she would boast: "I see my child so plainly; today he is more beautiful than yesterday." Angels bring light.

I remember a scene in Poland. Standing in a typical, pure white chancel, focused on a medieval crucifix, I heard someone with a camera say to her friend, a fellow traveler, "Please move. You are standing between me and Jesus." The woman between her friend and the crucifix began to scream. She thought that she was not only blocking the view of the camera, but that she stood between her friend and Christ. She, with her body, blocked the view; angels as spirit would glorify the view.

Angels do not hide Jesus; they cast light on Jesus. They throng the air.

God, your angels throng the air
Left and right and everywhere
Now close my eyes and give me sight
To find them on my left and right
So much there is I do not see
Except by faith inside of me

But his mother only . . .

When sun has set and day is done
When all have left and I am one
Then God does wake inside my mind
The prayers of all humankind

"**His mother only.**" Jesus' mother was not a throng; she was one. A girl, unknown, whom Gabriel found in an obscure village and announced that she would bear the Messiah. She believed, and now in a town the was not home, she was the mother of Jesus, his mother only.

Did she have young siblings in her family whom she helped to raise? Did she know how to feed and diaper and dress and burp a baby? Surely mother Anna taught her these ways of her people. And she must have memorized by heart songs other than the Magnificat to sing while she rocked the Christ child.

Mary was his mother only, but she was not lonely. "Mary believed." The main gifts to be a mother were inside Mary. She knew who her baby was. Believing is not lonely.

Every mother is also a "mother only." Family and friends may gather, and the house may be full of gifts cuddling the child and the sharing of food and drink. Yet, a mother must know when she sees the child and nurses the baby that she is "mother only." What awesome awareness, to birth a child who will now live thirty, sixty, or ninety years of life on earth, and then eternal life. What father or mother does not ponder this while holding and rocking their own child.

Infant Jesus knew his mother more than he knew Joseph. A maid from the inn might want to help Mary, but the baby would not know a woman from the inn, not know a woman other than Mary. He would cry until he was back in Mary's arms. He would know by her aroma, for a mother's body is like incense to her newborn.

Mary in a sense stayed "his mother only." What an honor. Yet, I believe the words of Saint Francis that we should all want to be the mother of Jesus and have Christ in us.

She only believed
So great was the announcement
And then she conceived
And bore the world a sacrament
She only believed
Sometimes we only need say yes

In her maiden bliss . . .

A mother blush upon her face
A brush of tinted grace
And in the halo light that shone
She was a queen upon a throne
This girl of tinted grace

MARY HAD NOT BIRTHED BEFORE, AND THIS WAS NOT A
USUAL BIRTH. She started motherhood with a blush. Did she tell
her best friends what Gabriel had told her? Would she write it
in her daily diary? Would she lock the book and hide the key?
Did she look down as she told who this child was? Or did she
sing her Magnificat often, beaming as she told others face to face
about this birth?

Who has not seen bliss shine through the face of a very
young mother, glad for the birth yet surprised by this great wonder in her young life?

Bliss. It is easy to see Mary full of bliss: delight, elation,
ecstasy, rapture. She was on cloud nine. The antonym to bliss is
hell. Bliss. What Mary had in her defied hell and torment. So it is
to be with us. "Though devils all the world shall fill, they cannot
overpower us."

Have you noticed the blush in the face of a fifteen year old girl who is bringing a huge secret to pass on earth? Mary, a girl, was becoming an unforgettable character on earth. In her maiden bliss, she did not know this. She did not know of the masters' paintings and many carvings in wood and metal of the Madonna. She did not know of the many "Hail Marys" that would be recited in the next two thousand years. Mary was young and consumed in bliss.

I too blush when I feel this Christ in me. I too feel like skipping in springtime, knowing a great surprise has been given to me. I too am a blissful maiden or lad overflowing with wonder.

Ah the feeling of a first born
Finding life in me, romping
Then to leave one womb
To travel everywhere
And always being there
So may this Child be God's Amen
The one who came to Bethlehem

Worshipped the Beloved . . .

Nine months and here you are

Was the journey very far?

How is it to be a soul wrapped inside a human form?

Can you still remember, now that you are born?

IT IS A SACRED FEELING TO FACE A NEWBORN AND ASK

QUESTIONS. Where did you come from? Is there a place where God gives out souls and clothes them in a body? What do you know? Who are you already? What do you know about me? Does this world outside the womb feel strange, hostile, or welcoming? After asking the infant, I am in awe. The infant knows what I do not know and does not tell me. I am filled with reverence.

After Gabriel whispered the miracle to Mary, she must have been in great awe; awe is close to worship. Mary worshipped the Beloved. She knew who he was. She knew that Immanuel, this child, was God's promise to her people. I believe the words: "Mary believed." She did not comprehend; she believed, and so she worshipped. The angel knew more than she; now the child knew more than she. The child was of God and born of God's Spirit.

Why does a newborn intrigue us so? Why am I still so fascinated by Henry Frederick, a stillborn grandson, who never spoke or looked at me? How easy it was to write him an entire book (*To Henry in Heaven*) and still not be finished.

I do not worship Henry Frederick, but I ask him for answers I do not know. While I wrote, he drew me into the realm of truth that we find by faith. Henry took me over the line to heaven; Jesus crossed the line to earth. Nativity is a bridge between heaven and earth.

Mary worshipped the Beloved, another name for Jesus. I hope Mary heard a voice from heaven call her son "Beloved" at the Jordan. More than loved, he is beloved.

> *God, I ask for I do not know*
> *And believing makes it more than so*
> *God, I ask, still you do not tell*
> *For I would not comprehend you very well*
> *God, I ask; you teach me how to trust*
> *You tell me only what you must*
> *So with Mary I say so be it, I believe*

With a kiss.

What child has not felt the joy of parent touch
A kiss, the words: I love you very much?
What child has not found its holy place
In a warm and sudden kiss of grace?

MARY WORSHIPPED JESUS WITH A KISS. More than one kiss,
many, and more. A kiss while angels sang about peace on earth
and shepherds bowed and told Mary what had happened in the
skies. A kiss of peace. This kiss has been treasured by the church.
We have kept the kiss as part of worship, the *Pax*, the kiss of peace.

For some the kiss is a handshake in worship, for some a
wave, for some a look into the eyes to see the soul of the other.
Luther said we are to see Christ in our neighbor. So in the passing of the peace we see Christ in the other. Stay long enough in
the passing of the peace, the *Pax*, to see Christ. It is Christ you
are kissing and who is kissing you.

In a Navy retreat center, I met with twenty chaplains for
a week. One session was all about holiness. I asked each chap-
lain to take us to a most holy place, a most worshipful moment.
They took us to rivers, pulpits, Mack trucks, hospitals, and altars.

A priest created for our imagination an altar of three thousand pounds of rock from many places. He thought he had finished. We could all imagine the altar. Then I asked him to kiss the altar. He did, at the left corner near him. He had not taken us to his most holy place. I asked where his lips were. He said Jerusalem, for the rock was from there. The rabbi cheered. I asked him three more times to kiss the corner of the altar and tell me what his lips were touching. I can still hear him: a relic, the Eucharist in the catacombs, Christ! Kissing Christ was the kiss of peace. He did what Mary did: she worshipped with a kiss. Then he passed the kiss to all of us. Mary kissed the Christ. So do we; that is the *Pax*.

O Christ, the stable lost its hay
Souvenirs to those who came to pray
The stable is now empty
Gave itself away
We kiss each other, the kiss is quite the same
We kiss the Christ, we kiss in Jesus' name
We give ourselves away; it is the same

What shall I give Him?...

THE FINAL VERSE OF THE HYMN IS THE MOST WELL-KNOWN AND -LOVED. Now we are drawn into the stable. Angels, archangels, Mary, Joseph—all have given the child a gift. What shall I give? What does he need? Or, what do I need to give? What do I want to give? What am I able to give? What does he ask me to give? Which is it?

I saw an Orthodox woman in Russia give devotion. For hours she stood motionless before an icon of Jesus and gave herself. Standing there, it seemed she gave nothing. She only received. It was as though this old iconic painting wrapped around her and pierced her spirit and fed her with all of Christ. She was giving herself to Jesus' glory. She was surrendering completely and looked saved. As she gave herself, she received. What shall I give him? Devotion.

In the streets of Erfurt I saw a Pieta, Mary holding her deceased son in her lap. It was in a church niche along a busy street, which people have passed by for four hundred years. Jesus' right thumb was shiny. It had received countless kisses by passersby through the centuries. Mary's kiss is alive. What shall I give? The kiss of peace.

Judas kissed Jesus in the garden. "The one you want is the one I kiss." This kiss of betrayal was not a kiss of peace. Though at that moment Jesus called him "friend." Perhaps this was a kiss of friendship. Perhaps Judas did expect Jesus finally to show his power and glory and do miracles to set the people free. Jesus had come to set another kingdom free, the kingdom of spirit, soul, mind, heart. It is a kingdom hidden. We see the kingdom and don't see; we hear and don't hear. What shall I give him? Eyes to see, ears to hear.

The *Pax* in the chaplains' school was hidden inside the huge altar. Only as we studied the altar with the priest for many minutes did we get past the stone and beauty and splendor and relic. As we looked and thought deeper and deeper into the altar we found the "sign and symbol" of Christ. As always, Christ was concealed and revealed in a sacred sign. What shall I give? A deeper look.

God is hidden in Christ. Inside, in Christ, we find the peace, and then we pass it to each other and find it in each other. What shall I give him? The gift of peace he gives me. I will give this gift to another.

God, you hide and we are to find you
We close our eyes; give us a clue
Like children we seek in all places
As we seek it's sure to be you

So in faith I come to the manger
What is the gift that I give?
That my eyes and ears be quite open
And I find what you give me to live

Poor as I am?...

Were I poor, I would know
What I am to give
The gift I'd choose, I know, I know
Is bread, the bread I need to live
The child, the child is now my living bread
As he once said, as he once said

WHAT HAVE WE TO GIVE? Something? Everything?

I read a devotion that reminded readers it was a leap year. This means one extra day. The writer suggested that the reader give this extra day to someone as a gift. We have been given a free day, now give it to another. So what was given that we now give? A day.

What if someone poor gave me a full day?

Have you seen the eyes of the poor when given more than they can eat? Their eyes shine. The poor can see beyond what is in front of them. A whole baked potato or partially eaten sandwich is a feast. I have seen the poor eat a small piece of bread with both hands. The poor know the size of a gift. A widow's mite is more than they can afford. What if I gave the poor one whole day to give away?

We are poor when standing before a king or queen. We are poor when standing before the King of kings and Lord of lords. But the one in the manger does not see us as poor. He is as poor as we, and dependent on his mother for life, an infant, helpless, needful, poor, yet of God. We too are of God, queens and kings, a royal people. So what do poor people give God?

My children gave me homemade things. Scribbles, valentines, hand-drawn letters, colored hearts, sealed envelopes with loving notes inside, special stones with pretty markings, a feather, walnuts autographed with special words. Each Christmas season as a child, I gave my mother a gift. It was never something I bought, for I do not recall having spending money. I was poor and always had a good gift, a homemade gift. The poor have their own shopping mall.

What if someone poor gave me one full day? What kind of gift would that be?

O children, show me how to be poor

Give me your scribbles and homemade valentines

Find me a bumpy stone or broken glass that shines

Give me a hug, you know just how to hug

Show me your friend, a tiny ladybug

None of these a gift that you did buy

Priceless, homemade, poor, that's why

If I were a shepherd . . .

If I were a shepherd
I'd loan him my own staff
We'd climb the highest mountain top
We'd play a flute duet and never stop
And laugh and laugh and laugh

To be a shepherd was a childhood dream. Then I could live in a homemade corral with sheep all around me. I would protect them with a rod or slingshot and lead them. I'd know each sheep by name, and they would know my voice. My brother Harold would help. All the pictures of Jesus the good shepherd would come true in me.

What could I give the Christ child? If I were little, I'd give him my best slingshot, homemade out of an inner tube from our '28 Chevy. The Y-shaped wood would be smooth as glass, and my initials would be carved near the bottom. This I'd give the Christ child.

I had two goats to give, and I knew goats were in the shepherd's flock. If I gave him a goat, this would be half my flock. That would be fifty percent, more than a tithe. If the gift went straight to Jesus, this would not be too much.

I like wood; since childhood I saw myself as a wood carver.
If I were a shepherd there would be many hand-carved staffs
in the corner of my cabin. I do have many walking sticks, and I
would carve one of them as a gift.

One walking stick is a young maple tree too quickly trans-
planted by my eager son. It did not grow long or live. It is taller
than I, waiting in the corner of my garage to be a special gift. I
would ask a woodcarver to carve it as gift for the Christ. Walking
canes are important to me; a good shepherd needs a very good staff.

I could give the infant a harmonica so we could play songs
together. I have five, and most are in mint condition though
twenty years old. They are waiting to make a first sound. We
practice shepherd songs.

Shepherds need time for musing. Were the shepherds aware
of the irony of their visit to the child? Did they see the contrast:
lowly shepherds and King of kings?

> *God, make me a shepherd and show me some sheep*
> *Lost in some pasture. I hear them bleat*
> *I hear the pleading; it's someone I know*
> *You are my shepherd and so I will go*
> *This is my gift: I will show them the stall*
> *Where there's grace for each one and there's room for us all*

I would bring a lamb . . .

I held my envelope with love and put it on the plate
I was a child back then so I could hardly wait
I thought I saw it move and breathe, just like a paschal lamb
I felt the breath was mine and the lamb was who I am

IF I WERE A REAL SHEPHERD I WOULD HAVE MORE THAN
TWO GOATS, SO I COULD BRING A LAMB. What kind of lamb? I
could bring a lamb that needs care, the smallest in the flock, one
born maimed. I saw such lambs in Mrs. Knippelmeyer's kitchen
getting special attention; one was born blind. I would bring a
wounded lamb.

Or, I could bring the strongest lamb in the flock, the one
always leaving its mother and ending in some corner of the
pasture, bleating to be found. A strong lamb, independent, and
often in trouble, a lamb that needs to be hunted and found and
brought back. The child and the lamb could talk about being lost,
forsaken, and found again.

In our country church I had the feeling not only of bringing a lamb but of being the lamb. I knew lambs by living just
north of a sheepfold. Lambs were completely honest; they did

not pretend. All this came alive for me as a child on Communion Sunday. Each time we sang the same hymn, and Lydia at the pump organ played slow so we felt the hymn deep inside. "Just as I am, without one plea, O Lamb of God, I come, I come." Lambs, I knew, were honest and trusting; so I came to the altar honest and trusting. I came as a lamb every communion Sunday. Like Jesus, I was a lamb.

What kind of lamb would I bring as shepherd? Perhaps the most gentle lamb. The lamb that follows the shepherd knows the voice by heart and stays close. The lamb would not be a problem sheep, but obedient. There was one lamb Eugene had just south of our country home. It did no wrong. Raising this lamb was a joy. I would give the child a joyful gift, a trusting, precious, gentle lamb.

Forty years ago Lois wrote a song that many children have sung. The song reminds us of our purpose in life.

Little Lamb, little Lamb, do you know who made you?
The green grass underfoot, the blue sky up above,
Was it God who sent you to teach us how to love?

If I were a wise man . . .

What is the gift a wise man would bring
A puzzle, a riddle, cantata to sing?
What would a wise man finally lay down
A manuscript, dream, or a gold crown?

IF I WERE A WISE MAN I WOULD GIVE THE CHILD THE FULL
WRITINGS OF MARTIN LUTHER, THE WORKS OF BACH, AND THE
WORKS OF SHAKESPEARE. I would want him to know one wise
man, a genius, a professor who set the church free to see Jesus.
I would mark certain pages, especially the sermons based on
the nativity. In my garage, I have stored tapes of speeches given
by famous professors describing the birth of Jesus. Surely Jesus
would like to hear what we have said two thousand years later.
Then he could shed light on what we know and don't know.

On my refrigerator I have children's drawings of Jesus' birth.
They are drawn with innocence and child wisdom. What a gift
this would be. I have seldom heard Jesus laugh. These pictures
would bring guffaws and more, I am sure. What a gift it would be
to make the Christ glad.

Many of my friends are fine musicians, brilliant, wise. I'd gather them into my house for a night of the finest song and music. If others heard, I'd invite more, and we'd schedule a time of music in the Basilica as a gift to the child. Then we could reserve the Minneapolis Auditorium, hopefully for many nights. All profits would go to the child's favorite charity.

If I were a wise man, I'd call Sweden and recommend Jesus for the Nobel Peace Prize. That would be my gift. And I'd invite all networks in the world to carry the presentation with the agreement that Jesus could speak as long as he wanted.

As a wise man I could tell Jesus my greatest dream and ask him to comment. I would face him and listen; this would be my greatest gift, to listen.

O God, I feel most wise
When I contemplate wisdom in disguise
What you told and we now ponder
We believe and then we wonder
Ah how much you did not say
On which we meditate each day
Is this our task, when we believe: to ask?

I would do my part . . .

"I WOULD DO MY PART" IS LIKE VOLUNTEERING. *Volentia*
and volunteering carry the meaning: "I will." What does a wise
man will to do? What is the legacy of a wise man?

Listen! Do you hear the handbells ringing in the cold,
welcoming people to give an offering, a donation for a need in
the world? Can you see the smiles, how each ringer finds a way
to meet your eyes so you do not look hurried and walk past the
black kettle as though it isn't there? By the time I am finished
shopping and buy everything on my shopping list, I am more
gracious; I put in a dollar. The ringers do not seem surprised.
They smile and thank me once more.

So when do I do my part? When do I give the dollar?
When is the gift enough, or right?

As a child I had a thought. Seeing the offering plate come
down the row, I took my little money and laid it into the basket
or cloth bag on the end of a long pole. The pole looked like a
fishing pole, and I saw Jesus fishing for more than money—for
us, for me. So began the thought of giving myself. What would
that look like? To me it meant leaving my father and mother and
going to a faraway land among strangers and telling stories of

Jesus. That is how I felt then, and I still do. I am to be the whole offering.

So what would a wise man or woman give? His instruments for reading stars? Manuscripts of wisdom and findings of scholars? Perhaps a castle his wisdom helped him purchase? The trophy for her Nobel Peace Prize? Would she quit work to become a missionary? Quit preaching to become a U.S. senator? Would he or she sing in the choir? When does a wise man or woman do her or his part? When is he or she in the offering plate?

When Lois died, I wanted to assume her role, and mine, as grandparent to five very young grandchildren. I bought things to take, to show, to eat, to read, to do. What could I do? What could I give and show and tell of a grandpa's wisdom? My health was poor, I was tired, I had little energy, I could not get down to play. How could I do my part? I found what they wanted most: for me to be there and see them play. To see them jumping rope and making sand castles. They wanted me to be with them. That was enough. They wanted me in the offering basket. Then I would be doing my part to be totally present.

He didn't leave us silver, gold or jasper, good perfume

But stories of a simple meal inside an upper room

He didn't leave us words on words and volumes that he said

But left us with a law of life: God raises from the dead

He didn't leave us wintry cold and not a spring in sight

But every day the promise: God wakes the morning light

Yet what I can I give Him . . .

THE GIFT I THOUGHT TO GIVE HIM MAY BE TOO BIG; THE GIFT MAY BE TOO SMALL. See what the shepherds and wise men gave. And see how they worshipped.

I have a ring I treasure, bought in Lübeck, Germany, in 1949. My wedding ring; I will give it to a grandson. It is a good gift. I would kneel to give the ring.

On my wall are oil paintings of great value to me, painted in a refugee camp, paintings of Lois and myself. They are heirlooms, but I could part with them. They are good gifts. I would bless them.

On a white oak shelf are books I have written in the past fifty years. They are being saved for the family. I believe they are good gifts. I want to know what they mean to Jesus. I would bow low.

A house in the Minnesota River valley is our family homestead. All the family has left the house to go into the city: Minneapolis, Tokyo, San Francisco. I have stayed; the house may soon be empty. There are memorial trees planted on all sides, with names and words marking family events. A grandson is under a maple. Childhood treasures and fifty years of family pets are buried in the hallowed earth. I could give this all to Jesus. What would the Christ child do with my house? I would give it for free.

There are watches I bought behind the Iron Curtain thirty years ago. They have never run. I am waiting for the right moment. Would these be a proper gift? What if Jesus would talk to me about time and space? I'll give him my father's watch from one hundred years ago. What will Jesus tell me about my father? I will hold it high like a gold offering.

Stored somewhere in the garage are tapes of young people speaking in many cities. I asked them to say what they saw when I read words like *grace* and *Jesus* and *faith* and *love* and *forgiveness* and *heaven*. Their imagination was unforgettable; it is recorded and stored in boxes. That was forty-five years ago. It is my gift. I would watch Jesus' face when he heard their answers. I would bow down.

What can I give him? All these, and more. Or, an apple tree in March, planted with the Lord's Prayer at its roots, outside my window. Very good.

> *She gave birth to her firstborn Son*
> *And it was good, very good*
> *Shepherds bowed, it was their gift*
> *As they should, as they should*
> *And it was good, very good*

Give my heart.

O God, we pray, O come into my heart
If there be any other part of me for you to be
Like feet or mind or liver or the spleen
Or some vital organ still unseen
Then come, O God, though be it very small
Come, as you came inside a tiny cattle stall

YET WHAT CAN I GIVE HIM? I can give him my heart. So what is the heart?

As a child we sang: "Come into my heart, Lord Jesus." Later I wrote hymns asking Jesus to come into my hands and feet and stomach and liver and lungs. Jesus heals from inside out, so I have often invited him into myself.

My heart is not well. I would rather give my brain or hands.

A child I knew imagined swallowing Jesus and having him in her heart. It was good for her to think of Jesus so up close, in the heart. She had no clue what the the heart does or looks like. I have heard mine often; it is a very loud and busy place. When she learned that swallowing leads to the stomach, she was disappointed. God was in her stomach. By now she has learned that she needs God in her heart and stomach, and in all inner places.

Psalm 139 makes this clear. The singer invites God into the womb and the innermost parts. Anyone who has been ill or in surgery or who is aging knows the comfort of God in us. A wonderful anthem has the words: "God be in my head and heart and in my understanding." Years ago I learned I have congestive heart failure. How often I have prayed that God be in my heart. Since, I have learned to give my heart to Jesus, along with my liver and kidney and lungs and veins. Christ is the healer, and I invite God into myself.

So what is the heart? The heart touches all parts. The heart is linked with every organ. As medicines heal my heart, doctors do regular tests on my liver, lungs, kidneys, pancreas, and stomach. My heart is also connected with my feelings and thoughts. Holding my breath can change my heart rate. A worry or a sudden joy can do the same. A song will change my blood pressure. So can prayer, silence, quiet, a snowfall.

What is the heart? Myself. I will give my heart. What is the heart? Myself.

In the bleak midwinter

In the silent cold

Beats a heart so warmly

As in eons old

'Tis the heart created

When earth was very new

Beating through all ages

Made for me and you

God has a heart that's beating

That lives inside of me

Where is my heart most gladsome?

In God's nativity